INFORMATION

NAME	
ADDRESS	
EMAIL	
PHONE	
MOBILE	

CLIENT RECORD

Client Name	Date	Page #	Date	Page #	Date	Page #	Date	Page #	Date	Page #
Client Name	Date	Page #	Date	Page #	Date	Page #	Date	Page #	Date	Page #

CLIENT RECORD

Client Name	Date	Page #	Date	Page #	Date	Page #	Date	Page #	Date	Page #

Client Name:		Date:
Contact Information:		
Meeting Time:	**Duration:**	

REFLECTION:

Where did we leave off? (Goals, concerns, or agreed upon action steps, etc.)

CLIENT CHECK-IN:

Progress or changes since last session, including experience with "homework":

SESSION GOALS:

Coach's main focus or goal(s) for today's session:

Client's main focus or goal(s) for today's session:

SESSION SUMMARY:

Main points discussed in session, including any updates to goals:

CLIENT HOMEWORK/ACTION STEPS:

COACH'S CORNER:

What went well in the session?

What challenges came up (for me or my client)?

What could I have done better or in what way can I improve?

What do I need to do to be prepared for next session?

Next session details:	DATE:	TIME:

NOTES

Client Name:	Date:

Contact Information:

Meeting Time:	Duration:

REFLECTION:

Where did we leave off? (Goals, concerns, or agreed upon action steps, etc.)

CLIENT CHECK-IN:

Progress or changes since last session, including experience with "homework":

SESSION GOALS:

Coach's main focus or goal(s) for today's session:

Client's main focus or goal(s) for today's session:

SESSION SUMMARY:

Main points discussed in session, including any updates to goals:

CLIENT HOMEWORK/ACTION STEPS:

COACH'S CORNER:

What went well in the session?

What challenges came up (for me or my client)?

What could I have done better or in what way can I improve?

What do I need to do to be prepared for next session?

Next session details: DATE: TIME:

NOTES

Client Name:	Date:

Contact Information:

Meeting Time:	Duration:

REFLECTION:

Where did we leave off? (Goals, concerns, or agreed upon action steps, etc.)

CLIENT CHECK-IN:

Progress or changes since last session, including experience with "homework":

SESSION GOALS:

Coach's main focus or goal(s) for today's session:

Client's main focus or goal(s) for today's session:

SESSION SUMMARY:

Main points discussed in session, including any updates to goals:

CLIENT HOMEWORK/ACTION STEPS:

COACH'S CORNER:

What went well in the session?

What challenges came up (for me or my client)?

What could I have done better or in what way can I improve?

What do I need to do to be prepared for next session?

Next session details: DATE: TIME:

NOTES

Client Name:	Date:

Contact Information:

Meeting Time:	Duration:

REFLECTION:

Where did we leave off? (Goals, concerns, or agreed upon action steps, etc.)

CLIENT CHECK-IN:

Progress or changes since last session, including experience with "homework":

SESSION GOALS:

Coach's main focus or goal(s) for today's session:

Client's main focus or goal(s) for today's session:

SESSION SUMMARY:

Main points discussed in session, including any updates to goals:

CLIENT HOMEWORK/ACTION STEPS:

COACH'S CORNER:

What went well in the session?

What challenges came up (for me or my client)?

What could I have done better or in what way can I improve?

What do I need to do to be prepared for next session?

Next session details: DATE: TIME:

NOTES

Client Name:	Date:

Contact Information:

Meeting Time:	Duration:

REFLECTION:

Where did we leave off? (Goals, concerns, or agreed upon action steps, etc.)

CLIENT CHECK-IN:

Progress or changes since last session, including experience with "homework":

SESSION GOALS:

Coach's main focus or goal(s) for today's session:

Client's main focus or goal(s) for today's session:

SESSION SUMMARY:

Main points discussed in session, including any updates to goals:

CLIENT HOMEWORK/ACTION STEPS:

COACH'S CORNER:

What went well in the session?

What challenges came up (for me or my client)?

What could I have done better or in what way can I improve?

What do I need to do to be prepared for next session?

Next session details: DATE: TIME:

NOTES

Client Name:		Date:
Contact Information:		
Meeting Time:	**Duration:**	

REFLECTION:

Where did we leave off? (Goals, concerns, or agreed upon action steps, etc.)

CLIENT CHECK-IN:

Progress or changes since last session, including experience with "homework":

SESSION GOALS:

Coach's main focus or goal(s) for today's session:

Client's main focus or goal(s) for today's session:

SESSION SUMMARY:

Main points discussed in session, including any updates to goals:

CLIENT HOMEWORK/ACTION STEPS:

COACH'S CORNER:

What went well in the session?

What challenges came up (for me or my client)?

What could I have done better or in what way can I improve?

What do I need to do to be prepared for next session?

Next session details: DATE: TIME:

NOTES

Client Name:	Date:

Contact Information:

Meeting Time:	Duration:

REFLECTION:

Where did we leave off? (Goals, concerns, or agreed upon action steps, etc.)

CLIENT CHECK-IN:

Progress or changes since last session, including experience with "homework":

SESSION GOALS:

Coach's main focus or goal(s) for today's session:

Client's main focus or goal(s) for today's session:

SESSION SUMMARY:

Main points discussed in session, including any updates to goals:

CLIENT HOMEWORK/ACTION STEPS:

COACH'S CORNER:

What went well in the session?

What challenges came up (for me or my client)?

What could I have done better or in what way can I improve?

What do I need to do to be prepared for next session?

Next session details: DATE: TIME:

NOTES

Client Name:		Date:

Contact Information:

Meeting Time:	Duration:

REFLECTION:

Where did we leave off? (Goals, concerns, or agreed upon action steps, etc.)

CLIENT CHECK-IN:

Progress or changes since last session, including experience with "homework":

SESSION GOALS:

Coach's main focus or goal(s) for today's session:

Client's main focus or goal(s) for today's session:

SESSION SUMMARY:

Main points discussed in session, including any updates to goals:

CLIENT HOMEWORK/ACTION STEPS:

COACH'S CORNER:

What went well in the session?

What challenges came up (for me or my client)?

What could I have done better or in what way can I improve?

What do I need to do to be prepared for next session?

Next session details: DATE: TIME:

NOTES

Client Name:		Date:
Contact Information:		
Meeting Time:	Duration:	

REFLECTION:

Where did we leave off? (Goals, concerns, or agreed upon action steps, etc.)

CLIENT CHECK-IN:

Progress or changes since last session, including experience with "homework":

SESSION GOALS:

Coach's main focus or goal(s) for today's session:

Client's main focus or goal(s) for today's session:

SESSION SUMMARY:

Main points discussed in session, including any updates to goals:

CLIENT HOMEWORK/ACTION STEPS:

COACH'S CORNER:

What went well in the session?

What challenges came up (for me or my client)?

What could I have done better or in what way can I improve?

What do I need to do to be prepared for next session?

Next session details: DATE: TIME:

NOTES

Client Name:	Date:

Contact Information:

Meeting Time:	Duration:

REFLECTION:

Where did we leave off? (Goals, concerns, or agreed upon action steps, etc.)

CLIENT CHECK-IN:

Progress or changes since last session, including experience with "homework":

SESSION GOALS:

Coach's main focus or goal(s) for today's session:

Client's main focus or goal(s) for today's session:

SESSION SUMMARY:

Main points discussed in session, including any updates to goals:

CLIENT HOMEWORK/ACTION STEPS:

COACH'S CORNER:

What went well in the session?

What challenges came up (for me or my client)?

What could I have done better or in what way can I improve?

What do I need to do to be prepared for next session?

Next session details: DATE: TIME:

NOTES

Client Name:	Date:

Contact Information:

Meeting Time:	Duration:

REFLECTION:

Where did we leave off? (Goals, concerns, or agreed upon action steps, etc.)

CLIENT CHECK-IN:

Progress or changes since last session, including experience with "homework":

SESSION GOALS:

Coach's main focus or goal(s) for today's session:

Client's main focus or goal(s) for today's session:

SESSION SUMMARY:

Main points discussed in session, including any updates to goals:

CLIENT HOMEWORK/ACTION STEPS:

COACH'S CORNER:

What went well in the session?

What challenges came up (for me or my client)?

What could I have done better or in what way can I improve?

What do I need to do to be prepared for next session?

Next session details: DATE: TIME:

NOTES

Client Name:	Date:

Contact Information:

Meeting Time: | **Duration:**

REFLECTION:

Where did we leave off? (Goals, concerns, or agreed upon action steps, etc.)

CLIENT CHECK-IN:

Progress or changes since last session, including experience with "homework":

SESSION GOALS:

Coach's main focus or goal(s) for today's session:

Client's main focus or goal(s) for today's session:

SESSION SUMMARY:

Main points discussed in session, including any updates to goals:

CLIENT HOMEWORK/ACTION STEPS:

COACH'S CORNER:

What went well in the session?

What challenges came up (for me or my client)?

What could I have done better or in what way can I improve?

What do I need to do to be prepared for next session?

Next session details: DATE: TIME:

NOTES

Client Name:	Date:

Contact Information:

Meeting Time:	Duration:

REFLECTION:

Where did we leave off? (Goals, concerns, or agreed upon action steps, etc.)

CLIENT CHECK-IN:

Progress or changes since last session, including experience with "homework":

SESSION GOALS:

Coach's main focus or goal(s) for today's session:

Client's main focus or goal(s) for today's session:

SESSION SUMMARY:

Main points discussed in session, including any updates to goals:

CLIENT HOMEWORK/ACTION STEPS:

COACH'S CORNER:

What went well in the session?

What challenges came up (for me or my client)?

What could I have done better or in what way can I improve?

What do I need to do to be prepared for next session?

Next session details: DATE: TIME:

NOTES

Client Name:	Date:

Contact Information:

Meeting Time:	Duration:

REFLECTION:

Where did we leave off? (Goals, concerns, or agreed upon action steps, etc.)

CLIENT CHECK-IN:

Progress or changes since last session, including experience with "homework":

SESSION GOALS:

Coach's main focus or goal(s) for today's session:

Client's main focus or goal(s) for today's session:

SESSION SUMMARY:

Main points discussed in session, including any updates to goals:

CLIENT HOMEWORK/ACTION STEPS:

COACH'S CORNER:

What went well in the session?

What challenges came up (for me or my client)?

What could I have done better or in what way can I improve?

What do I need to do to be prepared for next session?

Next session details: DATE: TIME:

NOTES

Client Name:	Date:

Contact Information:

Meeting Time:	Duration:

REFLECTION:

Where did we leave off? (Goals, concerns, or agreed upon action steps, etc.)

CLIENT CHECK-IN:

Progress or changes since last session, including experience with "homework":

SESSION GOALS:

Coach's main focus or goal(s) for today's session:

Client's main focus or goal(s) for today's session:

SESSION SUMMARY:

Main points discussed in session, including any updates to goals:

CLIENT HOMEWORK/ACTION STEPS:

COACH'S CORNER:

What went well in the session?

What challenges came up (for me or my client)?

What could I have done better or in what way can I improve?

What do I need to do to be prepared for next session?

Next session details: DATE: TIME:

NOTES

Client Name:	Date:

Contact Information:

Meeting Time:	Duration:

REFLECTION:

Where did we leave off? (Goals, concerns, or agreed upon action steps, etc.)

CLIENT CHECK-IN:

Progress or changes since last session, including experience with "homework":

SESSION GOALS:

Coach's main focus or goal(s) for today's session:

Client's main focus or goal(s) for today's session:

SESSION SUMMARY:

Main points discussed in session, including any updates to goals:

CLIENT HOMEWORK/ACTION STEPS:

COACH'S CORNER:

What went well in the session?

What challenges came up (for me or my client)?

What could I have done better or in what way can I improve?

What do I need to do to be prepared for next session?

Next session details: DATE: TIME:

NOTES

Client Name:	Date:

Contact Information:

Meeting Time: | **Duration:**

REFLECTION:

Where did we leave off? (Goals, concerns, or agreed upon action steps, etc.)

CLIENT CHECK-IN:

Progress or changes since last session, including experience with "homework":

SESSION GOALS:

Coach's main focus or goal(s) for today's session:

Client's main focus or goal(s) for today's session:

SESSION SUMMARY:

Main points discussed in session, including any updates to goals:

CLIENT HOMEWORK/ACTION STEPS:

COACH'S CORNER:

What went well in the session?

What challenges came up (for me or my client)?

What could I have done better or in what way can I improve?

What do I need to do to be prepared for next session?

Next session details: DATE: TIME:

NOTES

Client Name:	Date:

Contact Information:

Meeting Time:	Duration:

REFLECTION:

Where did we leave off? (Goals, concerns, or agreed upon action steps, etc.)

CLIENT CHECK-IN:

Progress or changes since last session, including experience with "homework":

SESSION GOALS:

Coach's main focus or goal(s) for today's session:

Client's main focus or goal(s) for today's session:

SESSION SUMMARY:

Main points discussed in session, including any updates to goals:

CLIENT HOMEWORK/ACTION STEPS:

COACH'S CORNER:

What went well in the session?

What challenges came up (for me or my client)?

What could I have done better or in what way can I improve?

What do I need to do to be prepared for next session?

Next session details: DATE: TIME:

NOTES

Client Name:	Date:

Contact Information:

Meeting Time:	Duration:

REFLECTION:

Where did we leave off? (Goals, concerns, or agreed upon action steps, etc.)

CLIENT CHECK-IN:

Progress or changes since last session, including experience with "homework":

SESSION GOALS:

Coach's main focus or goal(s) for today's session:

Client's main focus or goal(s) for today's session:

SESSION SUMMARY:

Main points discussed in session, including any updates to goals:

CLIENT HOMEWORK/ACTION STEPS:

COACH'S CORNER:

What went well in the session?

What challenges came up (for me or my client)?

What could I have done better or in what way can I improve?

What do I need to do to be prepared for next session?

Next session details: DATE: TIME:

NOTES

Client Name:		Date:
Contact Information:		

Meeting Time:	Duration:

REFLECTION:

Where did we leave off? (Goals, concerns, or agreed upon action steps, etc.)

CLIENT CHECK-IN:

Progress or changes since last session, including experience with "homework":

SESSION GOALS:

Coach's main focus or goal(s) for today's session:

Client's main focus or goal(s) for today's session:

SESSION SUMMARY:

Main points discussed in session, including any updates to goals:

CLIENT HOMEWORK/ACTION STEPS:

COACH'S CORNER:

What went well in the session?

What challenges came up (for me or my client)?

What could I have done better or in what way can I improve?

What do I need to do to be prepared for next session?

Next session details: DATE: TIME:

NOTES

Client Name:	Date:

Contact Information:

Meeting Time:	Duration:

REFLECTION:

Where did we leave off? (Goals, concerns, or agreed upon action steps, etc.)

CLIENT CHECK-IN:

Progress or changes since last session, including experience with "homework":

SESSION GOALS:

Coach's main focus or goal(s) for today's session:

Client's main focus or goal(s) for today's session:

SESSION SUMMARY:

Main points discussed in session, including any updates to goals:

CLIENT HOMEWORK/ACTION STEPS:

COACH'S CORNER:

What went well in the session?

What challenges came up (for me or my client)?

What could I have done better or in what way can I improve?

What do I need to do to be prepared for next session?

Next session details: DATE: TIME:

NOTES

Client Name:	Date:

Contact Information:

Meeting Time: | **Duration:**

REFLECTION:

Where did we leave off? (Goals, concerns, or agreed upon action steps, etc.)

CLIENT CHECK-IN:

Progress or changes since last session, including experience with "homework":

SESSION GOALS:

Coach's main focus or goal(s) for today's session:

Client's main focus or goal(s) for today's session:

SESSION SUMMARY:

Main points discussed in session, including any updates to goals:

CLIENT HOMEWORK/ACTION STEPS:

COACH'S CORNER:

What went well in the session?

What challenges came up (for me or my client)?

What could I have done better or in what way can I improve?

What do I need to do to be prepared for next session?

Next session details: DATE: TIME:

NOTES

Client Name:	Date:

Contact Information:

Meeting Time:	Duration:

REFLECTION:

Where did we leave off? (Goals, concerns, or agreed upon action steps, etc.)

CLIENT CHECK-IN:

Progress or changes since last session, including experience with "homework":

SESSION GOALS:

Coach's main focus or goal(s) for today's session:

Client's main focus or goal(s) for today's session:

SESSION SUMMARY:

Main points discussed in session, including any updates to goals:

CLIENT HOMEWORK/ACTION STEPS:

COACH'S CORNER:

What went well in the session?

What challenges came up (for me or my client)?

What could I have done better or in what way can I improve?

What do I need to do to be prepared for next session?

Next session details: DATE: TIME:

NOTES

Client Name:		Date:
Contact Information:		

Meeting Time:	Duration:

REFLECTION:

Where did we leave off? (Goals, concerns, or agreed upon action steps, etc.)

CLIENT CHECK-IN:

Progress or changes since last session, including experience with "homework":

SESSION GOALS:

Coach's main focus or goal(s) for today's session:

Client's main focus or goal(s) for today's session:

SESSION SUMMARY:

Main points discussed in session, including any updates to goals:

CLIENT HOMEWORK/ACTION STEPS:

COACH'S CORNER:

What went well in the session?

What challenges came up (for me or my client)?

What could I have done better or in what way can I improve?

What do I need to do to be prepared for next session?

Next session details: DATE: TIME:

NOTES

Client Name:	Date:

Contact Information:

Meeting Time:	Duration:

REFLECTION:

Where did we leave off? (Goals, concerns, or agreed upon action steps, etc.)

CLIENT CHECK-IN:

Progress or changes since last session, including experience with "homework":

SESSION GOALS:

Coach's main focus or goal(s) for today's session:

Client's main focus or goal(s) for today's session:

SESSION SUMMARY:

Main points discussed in session, including any updates to goals:

CLIENT HOMEWORK/ACTION STEPS:

COACH'S CORNER:

What went well in the session?

What challenges came up (for me or my client)?

What could I have done better or in what way can I improve?

What do I need to do to be prepared for next session?

Next session details: DATE: TIME:

NOTES

Client Name:	Date:

Contact Information:

Meeting Time:	Duration:

REFLECTION:

Where did we leave off? (Goals, concerns, or agreed upon action steps, etc.)

CLIENT CHECK-IN:

Progress or changes since last session, including experience with "homework":

SESSION GOALS:

Coach's main focus or goal(s) for today's session:

Client's main focus or goal(s) for today's session:

SESSION SUMMARY:

Main points discussed in session, including any updates to goals:

CLIENT HOMEWORK/ACTION STEPS:

COACH'S CORNER:

What went well in the session?

What challenges came up (for me or my client)?

What could I have done better or in what way can I improve?

What do I need to do to be prepared for next session?

Next session details: **DATE:**   **TIME:**

NOTES

Client Name:	Date:

Contact Information:

Meeting Time:	Duration:

REFLECTION:

Where did we leave off? (Goals, concerns, or agreed upon action steps, etc.)

CLIENT CHECK-IN:

Progress or changes since last session, including experience with "homework":

SESSION GOALS:

Coach's main focus or goal(s) for today's session:

Client's main focus or goal(s) for today's session:

SESSION SUMMARY:

Main points discussed in session, including any updates to goals:

CLIENT HOMEWORK/ACTION STEPS:

COACH'S CORNER:

What went well in the session?

What challenges came up (for me or my client)?

What could I have done better or in what way can I improve?

What do I need to do to be prepared for next session?

Next session details: DATE: TIME:

NOTES

Client Name:	Date:

Contact Information:

Meeting Time: | **Duration:**

REFLECTION:

Where did we leave off? (Goals, concerns, or agreed upon action steps, etc.)

CLIENT CHECK-IN:

Progress or changes since last session, including experience with "homework":

SESSION GOALS:

Coach's main focus or goal(s) for today's session:

Client's main focus or goal(s) for today's session:

SESSION SUMMARY:

Main points discussed in session, including any updates to goals:

CLIENT HOMEWORK/ACTION STEPS:

COACH'S CORNER:

What went well in the session?

What challenges came up (for me or my client)?

What could I have done better or in what way can I improve?

What do I need to do to be prepared for next session?

Next session details: DATE: TIME:

NOTES

Client Name:	Date:

Contact Information:

Meeting Time:	Duration:

REFLECTION:

Where did we leave off? (Goals, concerns, or agreed upon action steps, etc.)

CLIENT CHECK-IN:

Progress or changes since last session, including experience with "homework":

SESSION GOALS:

Coach's main focus or goal(s) for today's session:

Client's main focus or goal(s) for today's session:

SESSION SUMMARY:

Main points discussed in session, including any updates to goals:

CLIENT HOMEWORK/ACTION STEPS:

COACH'S CORNER:

What went well in the session?

What challenges came up (for me or my client)?

What could I have done better or in what way can I improve?

What do I need to do to be prepared for next session?

Next session details: DATE: TIME:

NOTES

Client Name:	Date:

Contact Information:

Meeting Time:	Duration:

REFLECTION:

Where did we leave off? (Goals, concerns, or agreed upon action steps, etc.)

CLIENT CHECK-IN:

Progress or changes since last session, including experience with "homework":

SESSION GOALS:

Coach's main focus or goal(s) for today's session:

Client's main focus or goal(s) for today's session:

SESSION SUMMARY:

Main points discussed in session, including any updates to goals:

CLIENT HOMEWORK/ACTION STEPS:

COACH'S CORNER:

What went well in the session?

What challenges came up (for me or my client)?

What could I have done better or in what way can I improve?

What do I need to do to be prepared for next session?

Next session details: DATE: TIME:

NOTES

Client Name:	Date:

Contact Information:

Meeting Time:	Duration:

REFLECTION:

Where did we leave off? (Goals, concerns, or agreed upon action steps, etc.)

CLIENT CHECK-IN:

Progress or changes since last session, including experience with "homework":

SESSION GOALS:

Coach's main focus or goal(s) for today's session:

Client's main focus or goal(s) for today's session:

SESSION SUMMARY:

Main points discussed in session, including any updates to goals:

CLIENT HOMEWORK/ACTION STEPS:

COACH'S CORNER:

What went well in the session?

What challenges came up (for me or my client)?

What could I have done better or in what way can I improve?

What do I need to do to be prepared for next session?

Next session details: DATE: TIME:

NOTES

Client Name:	Date:

Contact Information:

Meeting Time:	Duration:

REFLECTION:

Where did we leave off? (Goals, concerns, or agreed upon action steps, etc.)

CLIENT CHECK-IN:

Progress or changes since last session, including experience with "homework":

SESSION GOALS:

Coach's main focus or goal(s) for today's session:

Client's main focus or goal(s) for today's session:

SESSION SUMMARY:

Main points discussed in session, including any updates to goals:

CLIENT HOMEWORK/ACTION STEPS:

COACH'S CORNER:

What went well in the session?

What challenges came up (for me or my client)?

What could I have done better or in what way can I improve?

What do I need to do to be prepared for next session?

Next session details: DATE: TIME:

NOTES

Client Name:	Date:

Contact Information:

Meeting Time:	Duration:

REFLECTION:

Where did we leave off? (Goals, concerns, or agreed upon action steps, etc.)

CLIENT CHECK-IN:

Progress or changes since last session, including experience with "homework":

SESSION GOALS:

Coach's main focus or goal(s) for today's session:

Client's main focus or goal(s) for today's session:

SESSION SUMMARY:

Main points discussed in session, including any updates to goals:

CLIENT HOMEWORK/ACTION STEPS:

COACH'S CORNER:

What went well in the session?

What challenges came up (for me or my client)?

What could I have done better or in what way can I improve?

What do I need to do to be prepared for next session?

Next session details: DATE: TIME:

NOTES

Client Name:	Date:

Contact Information:

Meeting Time:	Duration:

REFLECTION:

Where did we leave off? (Goals, concerns, or agreed upon action steps, etc.)

CLIENT CHECK-IN:

Progress or changes since last session, including experience with "homework":

SESSION GOALS:

Coach's main focus or goal(s) for today's session:

Client's main focus or goal(s) for today's session:

SESSION SUMMARY:

Main points discussed in session, including any updates to goals:

CLIENT HOMEWORK/ACTION STEPS:

COACH'S CORNER:
What went well in the session?
What challenges came up (for me or my client)?
What could I have done better or in what way can I improve?
What do I need to do to be prepared for next session?

Next session details:	DATE:	TIME:

NOTES

Client Name:	Date:

Contact Information:

Meeting Time:	Duration:

REFLECTION:

Where did we leave off? (Goals, concerns, or agreed upon action steps, etc.)

CLIENT CHECK-IN:

Progress or changes since last session, including experience with "homework":

SESSION GOALS:

Coach's main focus or goal(s) for today's session:

Client's main focus or goal(s) for today's session:

SESSION SUMMARY:

Main points discussed in session, including any updates to goals:

CLIENT HOMEWORK/ACTION STEPS:

COACH'S CORNER:

What went well in the session?

What challenges came up (for me or my client)?

What could I have done better or in what way can I improve?

What do I need to do to be prepared for next session?

Next session details: DATE: TIME:

NOTES

Client Name:	Date:

Contact Information:

Meeting Time:	Duration:

REFLECTION:

Where did we leave off? (Goals, concerns, or agreed upon action steps, etc.)

CLIENT CHECK-IN:

Progress or changes since last session, including experience with "homework":

SESSION GOALS:

Coach's main focus or goal(s) for today's session:

Client's main focus or goal(s) for today's session:

SESSION SUMMARY:

Main points discussed in session, including any updates to goals:

CLIENT HOMEWORK/ACTION STEPS:

COACH'S CORNER:

What went well in the session?

What challenges came up (for me or my client)?

What could I have done better or in what way can I improve?

What do I need to do to be prepared for next session?

Next session details: DATE: TIME:

NOTES

Client Name:	Date:

Contact Information:

Meeting Time:	Duration:

REFLECTION:

Where did we leave off? (Goals, concerns, or agreed upon action steps, etc.)

CLIENT CHECK-IN:

Progress or changes since last session, including experience with "homework":

SESSION GOALS:

Coach's main focus or goal(s) for today's session:

Client's main focus or goal(s) for today's session:

SESSION SUMMARY:

Main points discussed in session, including any updates to goals:

CLIENT HOMEWORK/ACTION STEPS:

COACH'S CORNER:

What went well in the session?

What challenges came up (for me or my client)?

What could I have done better or in what way can I improve?

What do I need to do to be prepared for next session?

Next session details: DATE: TIME:

NOTES

Client Name:	Date:

Contact Information:

Meeting Time:	Duration:

REFLECTION:

Where did we leave off? (Goals, concerns, or agreed upon action steps, etc.)

CLIENT CHECK-IN:

Progress or changes since last session, including experience with "homework":

SESSION GOALS:

Coach's main focus or goal(s) for today's session:

Client's main focus or goal(s) for today's session:

SESSION SUMMARY:

Main points discussed in session, including any updates to goals:

CLIENT HOMEWORK/ACTION STEPS:

COACH'S CORNER:

What went well in the session?

What challenges came up (for me or my client)?

What could I have done better or in what way can I improve?

What do I need to do to be prepared for next session?

Next session details: DATE: TIME:

NOTES

Client Name:	Date:
Contact Information:	

Meeting Time:	Duration:

REFLECTION:

Where did we leave off? (Goals, concerns, or agreed upon action steps, etc.)

CLIENT CHECK-IN:

Progress or changes since last session, including experience with "homework":

SESSION GOALS:

Coach's main focus or goal(s) for today's session:

Client's main focus or goal(s) for today's session:

SESSION SUMMARY:

Main points discussed in session, including any updates to goals:

CLIENT HOMEWORK/ACTION STEPS:

COACH'S CORNER:

What went well in the session?

What challenges came up (for me or my client)?

What could I have done better or in what way can I improve?

What do I need to do to be prepared for next session?

Next session details: DATE: TIME:

NOTES

Client Name:	Date:

Contact Information:

Meeting Time:	Duration:

REFLECTION:

Where did we leave off? (Goals, concerns, or agreed upon action steps, etc.)

CLIENT CHECK-IN:

Progress or changes since last session, including experience with "homework":

SESSION GOALS:

Coach's main focus or goal(s) for today's session:

Client's main focus or goal(s) for today's session:

SESSION SUMMARY:

Main points discussed in session, including any updates to goals:

CLIENT HOMEWORK/ACTION STEPS:

COACH'S CORNER:

What went well in the session?

What challenges came up (for me or my client)?

What could I have done better or in what way can I improve?

What do I need to do to be prepared for next session?

Next session details: DATE: TIME:

NOTES

Client Name:	Date:

Contact Information:

Meeting Time: | **Duration:**

REFLECTION:

Where did we leave off? (Goals, concerns, or agreed upon action steps, etc.)

CLIENT CHECK-IN:

Progress or changes since last session, including experience with "homework":

SESSION GOALS:

Coach's main focus or goal(s) for today's session:

Client's main focus or goal(s) for today's session:

SESSION SUMMARY:

Main points discussed in session, including any updates to goals:

CLIENT HOMEWORK/ACTION STEPS:

COACH'S CORNER:

What went well in the session?

What challenges came up (for me or my client)?

What could I have done better or in what way can I improve?

What do I need to do to be prepared for next session?

Next session details: DATE: TIME:

NOTES

Client Name:	Date:

Contact Information:

Meeting Time:	Duration:

REFLECTION:

Where did we leave off? (Goals, concerns, or agreed upon action steps, etc.)

CLIENT CHECK-IN:

Progress or changes since last session, including experience with "homework":

SESSION GOALS:

Coach's main focus or goal(s) for today's session:

Client's main focus or goal(s) for today's session:

SESSION SUMMARY:

Main points discussed in session, including any updates to goals:

CLIENT HOMEWORK/ACTION STEPS:

COACH'S CORNER:

What went well in the session?

What challenges came up (for me or my client)?

What could I have done better or in what way can I improve?

What do I need to do to be prepared for next session?

Next session details: DATE: TIME:

NOTES

Client Name:	Date:

Contact Information:

Meeting Time:	Duration:

REFLECTION:

Where did we leave off? (Goals, concerns, or agreed upon action steps, etc.)

CLIENT CHECK-IN:

Progress or changes since last session, including experience with "homework":

SESSION GOALS:

Coach's main focus or goal(s) for today's session:

Client's main focus or goal(s) for today's session:

SESSION SUMMARY:

Main points discussed in session, including any updates to goals:

CLIENT HOMEWORK/ACTION STEPS:

COACH'S CORNER:

What went well in the session?

What challenges came up (for me or my client)?

What could I have done better or in what way can I improve?

What do I need to do to be prepared for next session?

Next session details: DATE: TIME:

NOTES

Client Name:	Date:

Contact Information:

Meeting Time:	Duration:

REFLECTION:

Where did we leave off? (Goals, concerns, or agreed upon action steps, etc.)

CLIENT CHECK-IN:

Progress or changes since last session, including experience with "homework":

SESSION GOALS:

Coach's main focus or goal(s) for today's session:

Client's main focus or goal(s) for today's session:

SESSION SUMMARY:

Main points discussed in session, including any updates to goals:

CLIENT HOMEWORK/ACTION STEPS:

COACH'S CORNER:

What went well in the session?

What challenges came up (for me or my client)?

What could I have done better or in what way can I improve?

What do I need to do to be prepared for next session?

Next session details: DATE: TIME:

NOTES

Client Name:	Date:

Contact Information:

Meeting Time: | **Duration:**

REFLECTION:

Where did we leave off? (Goals, concerns, or agreed upon action steps, etc.)

CLIENT CHECK-IN:

Progress or changes since last session, including experience with "homework":

SESSION GOALS:

Coach's main focus or goal(s) for today's session:

Client's main focus or goal(s) for today's session:

SESSION SUMMARY:

Main points discussed in session, including any updates to goals:

CLIENT HOMEWORK/ACTION STEPS:

COACH'S CORNER:

What went well in the session?

What challenges came up (for me or my client)?

What could I have done better or in what way can I improve?

What do I need to do to be prepared for next session?

Next session details: DATE: TIME:

NOTES

Client Name:	Date:

Contact Information:

Meeting Time:	Duration:

REFLECTION:

Where did we leave off? (Goals, concerns, or agreed upon action steps, etc.)

CLIENT CHECK-IN:

Progress or changes since last session, including experience with "homework":

SESSION GOALS:

Coach's main focus or goal(s) for today's session:

Client's main focus or goal(s) for today's session:

SESSION SUMMARY:

Main points discussed in session, including any updates to goals:

CLIENT HOMEWORK/ACTION STEPS:

COACH'S CORNER:

What went well in the session?

What challenges came up (for me or my client)?

What could I have done better or in what way can I improve?

What do I need to do to be prepared for next session?

Next session details: DATE: TIME:

NOTES

Client Name:	Date:

Contact Information:

Meeting Time:	Duration:

REFLECTION:

Where did we leave off? (Goals, concerns, or agreed upon action steps, etc.)

CLIENT CHECK-IN:

Progress or changes since last session, including experience with "homework":

SESSION GOALS:

Coach's main focus or goal(s) for today's session:

Client's main focus or goal(s) for today's session:

SESSION SUMMARY:

Main points discussed in session, including any updates to goals:

CLIENT HOMEWORK/ACTION STEPS:

COACH'S CORNER:

What went well in the session?

What challenges came up (for me or my client)?

What could I have done better or in what way can I improve?

What do I need to do to be prepared for next session?

Next session details: DATE: TIME:

NOTES

Client Name:	Date:

Contact Information:

Meeting Time:	Duration:

REFLECTION:

Where did we leave off? (Goals, concerns, or agreed upon action steps, etc.)

CLIENT CHECK-IN:

Progress or changes since last session, including experience with "homework":

SESSION GOALS:

Coach's main focus or goal(s) for today's session:

Client's main focus or goal(s) for today's session:

SESSION SUMMARY:

Main points discussed in session, including any updates to goals:

CLIENT HOMEWORK/ACTION STEPS:

COACH'S CORNER:

What went well in the session?

What challenges came up (for me or my client)?

What could I have done better or in what way can I improve?

What do I need to do to be prepared for next session?

Next session details: DATE: TIME:

NOTES

Client Name:	Date:

Contact Information:

Meeting Time:	Duration:

REFLECTION:

Where did we leave off? (Goals, concerns, or agreed upon action steps, etc.)

CLIENT CHECK-IN:

Progress or changes since last session, including experience with "homework":

SESSION GOALS:

Coach's main focus or goal(s) for today's session:

Client's main focus or goal(s) for today's session:

SESSION SUMMARY:

Main points discussed in session, including any updates to goals:

CLIENT HOMEWORK/ACTION STEPS:

COACH'S CORNER:

What went well in the session?

What challenges came up (for me or my client)?

What could I have done better or in what way can I improve?

What do I need to do to be prepared for next session?

Next session details: DATE: TIME:

NOTES

Client Name:		Date:
Contact Information:		
Meeting Time:	Duration:	

REFLECTION:

Where did we leave off? (Goals, concerns, or agreed upon action steps, etc.)

CLIENT CHECK-IN:

Progress or changes since last session, including experience with "homework":

SESSION GOALS:

Coach's main focus or goal(s) for today's session:

Client's main focus or goal(s) for today's session:

SESSION SUMMARY:

Main points discussed in session, including any updates to goals:

CLIENT HOMEWORK/ACTION STEPS:

COACH'S CORNER:

What went well in the session?

What challenges came up (for me or my client)?

What could I have done better or in what way can I improve?

What do I need to do to be prepared for next session?

Next session details: DATE: TIME:

NOTES

Client Name:	Date:

Contact Information:

Meeting Time:	Duration:

REFLECTION:

Where did we leave off? (Goals, concerns, or agreed upon action steps, etc.)

CLIENT CHECK-IN:

Progress or changes since last session, including experience with "homework":

SESSION GOALS:

Coach's main focus or goal(s) for today's session:

Client's main focus or goal(s) for today's session:

SESSION SUMMARY:

Main points discussed in session, including any updates to goals:

CLIENT HOMEWORK/ACTION STEPS:

COACH'S CORNER:

What went well in the session?

What challenges came up (for me or my client)?

What could I have done better or in what way can I improve?

What do I need to do to be prepared for next session?

Next session details: DATE: TIME:

NOTES

Client Name:	Date:

Contact Information:

Meeting Time:	Duration:

REFLECTION:

Where did we leave off? (Goals, concerns, or agreed upon action steps, etc.)

CLIENT CHECK-IN:

Progress or changes since last session, including experience with "homework":

SESSION GOALS:

Coach's main focus or goal(s) for today's session:

Client's main focus or goal(s) for today's session:

SESSION SUMMARY:

Main points discussed in session, including any updates to goals:

CLIENT HOMEWORK/ACTION STEPS:

COACH'S CORNER:

What went well in the session?

What challenges came up (for me or my client)?

What could I have done better or in what way can I improve?

What do I need to do to be prepared for next session?

Next session details: DATE: TIME:

NOTES

Client Name:	Date:

Contact Information:

Meeting Time:	Duration:

REFLECTION:

Where did we leave off? (Goals, concerns, or agreed upon action steps, etc.)

CLIENT CHECK-IN:

Progress or changes since last session, including experience with "homework":

SESSION GOALS:

Coach's main focus or goal(s) for today's session:

Client's main focus or goal(s) for today's session:

SESSION SUMMARY:

Main points discussed in session, including any updates to goals:

CLIENT HOMEWORK/ACTION STEPS:

COACH'S CORNER:

What went well in the session?

What challenges came up (for me or my client)?

What could I have done better or in what way can I improve?

What do I need to do to be prepared for next session?

Next session details: DATE: TIME:

NOTES

Client Name:		Date:

Contact Information:

Meeting Time:	Duration:

REFLECTION:

Where did we leave off? (Goals, concerns, or agreed upon action steps, etc.)

CLIENT CHECK-IN:

Progress or changes since last session, including experience with "homework":

SESSION GOALS:

Coach's main focus or goal(s) for today's session:

Client's main focus or goal(s) for today's session:

SESSION SUMMARY:

Main points discussed in session, including any updates to goals:

CLIENT HOMEWORK/ACTION STEPS:

COACH'S CORNER:

What went well in the session?

What challenges came up (for me or my client)?

What could I have done better or in what way can I improve?

What do I need to do to be prepared for next session?

Next session details: DATE: TIME:

NOTES

Client Name:	Date:

Contact Information:

Meeting Time:	Duration:

REFLECTION:

Where did we leave off? (Goals, concerns, or agreed upon action steps, etc.)

CLIENT CHECK-IN:

Progress or changes since last session, including experience with "homework":

SESSION GOALS:

Coach's main focus or goal(s) for today's session:

Client's main focus or goal(s) for today's session:

SESSION SUMMARY:

Main points discussed in session, including any updates to goals:

CLIENT HOMEWORK/ACTION STEPS:

COACH'S CORNER:

What went well in the session?

What challenges came up (for me or my client)?

What could I have done better or in what way can I improve?

What do I need to do to be prepared for next session?

Next session details: DATE: TIME:

NOTES

Client Name:		Date:
Contact Information:		

Meeting Time:	Duration:

REFLECTION:

Where did we leave off? (Goals, concerns, or agreed upon action steps, etc.)

CLIENT CHECK-IN:

Progress or changes since last session, including experience with "homework":

SESSION GOALS:

Coach's main focus or goal(s) for today's session:

Client's main focus or goal(s) for today's session:

SESSION SUMMARY:

Main points discussed in session, including any updates to goals:

CLIENT HOMEWORK/ACTION STEPS:

COACH'S CORNER:

What went well in the session?

What challenges came up (for me or my client)?

What could I have done better or in what way can I improve?

What do I need to do to be prepared for next session?

Next session details: DATE: TIME:

NOTES

Client Name:	Date:

Contact Information:

Meeting Time:	Duration:

REFLECTION:

Where did we leave off? (Goals, concerns, or agreed upon action steps, etc.)

CLIENT CHECK-IN:

Progress or changes since last session, including experience with "homework":

SESSION GOALS:

Coach's main focus or goal(s) for today's session:

Client's main focus or goal(s) for today's session:

SESSION SUMMARY:

Main points discussed in session, including any updates to goals:

CLIENT HOMEWORK/ACTION STEPS:

COACH'S CORNER:

What went well in the session?

What challenges came up (for me or my client)?

What could I have done better or in what way can I improve?

What do I need to do to be prepared for next session?

Next session details: DATE: TIME:

NOTES

Client Name:	Date:

Contact Information:

Meeting Time:	Duration:

REFLECTION:

Where did we leave off? (Goals, concerns, or agreed upon action steps, etc.)

CLIENT CHECK-IN:

Progress or changes since last session, including experience with "homework":

SESSION GOALS:

Coach's main focus or goal(s) for today's session:

Client's main focus or goal(s) for today's session:

SESSION SUMMARY:

Main points discussed in session, including any updates to goals:

CLIENT HOMEWORK/ACTION STEPS:

COACH'S CORNER:

What went well in the session?

What challenges came up (for me or my client)?

What could I have done better or in what way can I improve?

What do I need to do to be prepared for next session?

Next session details: DATE: TIME:

NOTES

Client Name:	Date:

Contact Information:

Meeting Time:	Duration:

REFLECTION:

Where did we leave off? (Goals, concerns, or agreed upon action steps, etc.)

CLIENT CHECK-IN:

Progress or changes since last session, including experience with "homework":

SESSION GOALS:

Coach's main focus or goal(s) for today's session:

Client's main focus or goal(s) for today's session:

SESSION SUMMARY:

Main points discussed in session, including any updates to goals:

CLIENT HOMEWORK/ACTION STEPS:

COACH'S CORNER:

What went well in the session?

What challenges came up (for me or my client)?

What could I have done better or in what way can I improve?

What do I need to do to be prepared for next session?

Next session details: DATE: TIME:

NOTES

Client Name:		Date:
Contact Information:		

Meeting Time:	Duration:

REFLECTION:

Where did we leave off? (Goals, concerns, or agreed upon action steps, etc.)

CLIENT CHECK-IN:

Progress or changes since last session, including experience with "homework":

SESSION GOALS:

Coach's main focus or goal(s) for today's session:

Client's main focus or goal(s) for today's session:

SESSION SUMMARY:

Main points discussed in session, including any updates to goals:

CLIENT HOMEWORK/ACTION STEPS:

COACH'S CORNER:

What went well in the session?

What challenges came up (for me or my client)?

What could I have done better or in what way can I improve?

What do I need to do to be prepared for next session?

Next session details: DATE: TIME:

NOTES

Client Name:	Date:

Contact Information:

Meeting Time:	Duration:

REFLECTION:

Where did we leave off? (Goals, concerns, or agreed upon action steps, etc.)

CLIENT CHECK-IN:

Progress or changes since last session, including experience with "homework":

SESSION GOALS:

Coach's main focus or goal(s) for today's session:

Client's main focus or goal(s) for today's session:

SESSION SUMMARY:

Main points discussed in session, including any updates to goals:

CLIENT HOMEWORK/ACTION STEPS:

COACH'S CORNER:

What went well in the session?

What challenges came up (for me or my client)?

What could I have done better or in what way can I improve?

What do I need to do to be prepared for next session?

Next session details: DATE: TIME:

NOTES

Client Name:	Date:

Contact Information:

Meeting Time:	Duration:

REFLECTION:

Where did we leave off? (Goals, concerns, or agreed upon action steps, etc.)

CLIENT CHECK-IN:

Progress or changes since last session, including experience with "homework":

SESSION GOALS:

Coach's main focus or goal(s) for today's session:

Client's main focus or goal(s) for today's session:

SESSION SUMMARY:

Main points discussed in session, including any updates to goals:

CLIENT HOMEWORK/ACTION STEPS:

COACH'S CORNER:

What went well in the session?

What challenges came up (for me or my client)?

What could I have done better or in what way can I improve?

What do I need to do to be prepared for next session?

Next session details: DATE: TIME:

NOTES

Client Name:	Date:

Contact Information:

Meeting Time: | **Duration:**

REFLECTION:

Where did we leave off? (Goals, concerns, or agreed upon action steps, etc.)

CLIENT CHECK-IN:

Progress or changes since last session, including experience with "homework":

SESSION GOALS:

Coach's main focus or goal(s) for today's session:

Client's main focus or goal(s) for today's session:

SESSION SUMMARY:

Main points discussed in session, including any updates to goals:

CLIENT HOMEWORK/ACTION STEPS:

COACH'S CORNER:

What went well in the session?

What challenges came up (for me or my client)?

What could I have done better or in what way can I improve?

What do I need to do to be prepared for next session?

Next session details: DATE: TIME:

NOTES

Client Name:	Date:

Contact Information:

Meeting Time:	Duration:

REFLECTION:

Where did we leave off? (Goals, concerns, or agreed upon action steps, etc.)

CLIENT CHECK-IN:

Progress or changes since last session, including experience with "homework":

SESSION GOALS:

Coach's main focus or goal(s) for today's session:

Client's main focus or goal(s) for today's session:

SESSION SUMMARY:

Main points discussed in session, including any updates to goals:

CLIENT HOMEWORK/ACTION STEPS:

COACH'S CORNER:

What went well in the session?

What challenges came up (for me or my client)?

What could I have done better or in what way can I improve?

What do I need to do to be prepared for next session?

Next session details: DATE: TIME:

NOTES

Client Name:	Date:

Contact Information:

Meeting Time:	Duration:

REFLECTION:

Where did we leave off? (Goals, concerns, or agreed upon action steps, etc.)

CLIENT CHECK-IN:

Progress or changes since last session, including experience with "homework":

SESSION GOALS:

Coach's main focus or goal(s) for today's session:

Client's main focus or goal(s) for today's session:

SESSION SUMMARY:

Main points discussed in session, including any updates to goals:

CLIENT HOMEWORK/ACTION STEPS:

COACH'S CORNER:

What went well in the session?

What challenges came up (for me or my client)?

What could I have done better or in what way can I improve?

What do I need to do to be prepared for next session?

Next session details: DATE: TIME:

NOTES

Client Name:		Date:
Contact Information:		

Meeting Time:	Duration:

REFLECTION:

Where did we leave off? (Goals, concerns, or agreed upon action steps, etc.)

CLIENT CHECK-IN:

Progress or changes since last session, including experience with "homework":

SESSION GOALS:

Coach's main focus or goal(s) for today's session:

Client's main focus or goal(s) for today's session:

SESSION SUMMARY:

Main points discussed in session, including any updates to goals:

CLIENT HOMEWORK/ACTION STEPS:

COACH'S CORNER:

What went well in the session?

What challenges came up (for me or my client)?

What could I have done better or in what way can I improve?

What do I need to do to be prepared for next session?

Next session details: DATE: TIME:

NOTES

Client Name:	Date:

Contact Information:

Meeting Time:	Duration:

REFLECTION:

Where did we leave off? (Goals, concerns, or agreed upon action steps, etc.)

CLIENT CHECK-IN:

Progress or changes since last session, including experience with "homework":

SESSION GOALS:

Coach's main focus or goal(s) for today's session:

Client's main focus or goal(s) for today's session:

SESSION SUMMARY:

Main points discussed in session, including any updates to goals:

CLIENT HOMEWORK/ACTION STEPS:

COACH'S CORNER:

What went well in the session?

What challenges came up (for me or my client)?

What could I have done better or in what way can I improve?

What do I need to do to be prepared for next session?

Next session details: DATE: TIME:

NOTES

Client Name:	Date:

Contact Information:

Meeting Time:	Duration:

REFLECTION:

Where did we leave off? (Goals, concerns, or agreed upon action steps, etc.)

CLIENT CHECK-IN:

Progress or changes since last session, including experience with "homework":

SESSION GOALS:

Coach's main focus or goal(s) for today's session:

Client's main focus or goal(s) for today's session:

SESSION SUMMARY:

Main points discussed in session, including any updates to goals:

CLIENT HOMEWORK/ACTION STEPS:

COACH'S CORNER:

What went well in the session?

What challenges came up (for me or my client)?

What could I have done better or in what way can I improve?

What do I need to do to be prepared for next session?

Next session details: DATE: TIME:

NOTES

Client Name:	Date:
Contact Information:	

Meeting Time:	Duration:

REFLECTION:

Where did we leave off? (Goals, concerns, or agreed upon action steps, etc.)

CLIENT CHECK-IN:

Progress or changes since last session, including experience with "homework":

SESSION GOALS:

Coach's main focus or goal(s) for today's session:

Client's main focus or goal(s) for today's session:

SESSION SUMMARY:

Main points discussed in session, including any updates to goals:

CLIENT HOMEWORK/ACTION STEPS:

COACH'S CORNER:

What went well in the session?

What challenges came up (for me or my client)?

What could I have done better or in what way can I improve?

What do I need to do to be prepared for next session?

Next session details: DATE: TIME:

NOTES

Client Name:	Date:

Contact Information:

Meeting Time:	Duration:

REFLECTION:

Where did we leave off? (Goals, concerns, or agreed upon action steps, etc.)

CLIENT CHECK-IN:

Progress or changes since last session, including experience with "homework":

SESSION GOALS:

Coach's main focus or goal(s) for today's session:

Client's main focus or goal(s) for today's session:

SESSION SUMMARY:

Main points discussed in session, including any updates to goals:

CLIENT HOMEWORK/ACTION STEPS:

COACH'S CORNER:

What went well in the session?

What challenges came up (for me or my client)?

What could I have done better or in what way can I improve?

What do I need to do to be prepared for next session?

Next session details: DATE: TIME:

NOTES

Client Name:	Date:

Contact Information:

Meeting Time: | **Duration:**

REFLECTION:

Where did we leave off? (Goals, concerns, or agreed upon action steps, etc.)

CLIENT CHECK-IN:

Progress or changes since last session, including experience with "homework":

SESSION GOALS:

Coach's main focus or goal(s) for today's session:

Client's main focus or goal(s) for today's session:

SESSION SUMMARY:

Main points discussed in session, including any updates to goals:

CLIENT HOMEWORK/ACTION STEPS:

COACH'S CORNER:

What went well in the session?

What challenges came up (for me or my client)?

What could I have done better or in what way can I improve?

What do I need to do to be prepared for next session?

Next session details: DATE: TIME:

NOTES

Client Name:	Date:

Contact Information:

Meeting Time:	Duration:

REFLECTION:

Where did we leave off? (Goals, concerns, or agreed upon action steps, etc.)

CLIENT CHECK-IN:

Progress or changes since last session, including experience with "homework":

SESSION GOALS:

Coach's main focus or goal(s) for today's session:

Client's main focus or goal(s) for today's session:

SESSION SUMMARY:

Main points discussed in session, including any updates to goals:

CLIENT HOMEWORK/ACTION STEPS:

COACH'S CORNER:

What went well in the session?

What challenges came up (for me or my client)?

What could I have done better or in what way can I improve?

What do I need to do to be prepared for next session?

Next session details: DATE: TIME:

NOTES

Client Name:	Date:

Contact Information:

Meeting Time:	Duration:

REFLECTION:

Where did we leave off? (Goals, concerns, or agreed upon action steps, etc.)

CLIENT CHECK-IN:

Progress or changes since last session, including experience with "homework":

SESSION GOALS:

Coach's main focus or goal(s) for today's session:

Client's main focus or goal(s) for today's session:

SESSION SUMMARY:

Main points discussed in session, including any updates to goals:

CLIENT HOMEWORK/ACTION STEPS:

COACH'S CORNER:

What went well in the session?

What challenges came up (for me or my client)?

What could I have done better or in what way can I improve?

What do I need to do to be prepared for next session?

Next session details: DATE: TIME:

NOTES

Client Name:	Date:

Contact Information:

Meeting Time:	Duration:

REFLECTION:

Where did we leave off? (Goals, concerns, or agreed upon action steps, etc.)

CLIENT CHECK-IN:

Progress or changes since last session, including experience with "homework":

SESSION GOALS:

Coach's main focus or goal(s) for today's session:

Client's main focus or goal(s) for today's session:

SESSION SUMMARY:

Main points discussed in session, including any updates to goals:

CLIENT HOMEWORK/ACTION STEPS:

COACH'S CORNER:

What went well in the session?

What challenges came up (for me or my client)?

What could I have done better or in what way can I improve?

What do I need to do to be prepared for next session?

Next session details: DATE: TIME:

NOTES

Client Name:	Date:

Contact Information:

Meeting Time:	Duration:

REFLECTION:

Where did we leave off? (Goals, concerns, or agreed upon action steps, etc.)

CLIENT CHECK-IN:

Progress or changes since last session, including experience with "homework":

SESSION GOALS:

Coach's main focus or goal(s) for today's session:

Client's main focus or goal(s) for today's session:

SESSION SUMMARY:

Main points discussed in session, including any updates to goals:

CLIENT HOMEWORK/ACTION STEPS:

COACH'S CORNER:

What went well in the session?

What challenges came up (for me or my client)?

What could I have done better or in what way can I improve?

What do I need to do to be prepared for next session?

Next session details: DATE: TIME:

NOTES

Client Name:		Date:

Contact Information:

Meeting Time:	Duration:

REFLECTION:

Where did we leave off? (Goals, concerns, or agreed upon action steps, etc.)

CLIENT CHECK-IN:

Progress or changes since last session, including experience with "homework":

SESSION GOALS:

Coach's main focus or goal(s) for today's session:

Client's main focus or goal(s) for today's session:

SESSION SUMMARY:

Main points discussed in session, including any updates to goals:

CLIENT HOMEWORK/ACTION STEPS:

COACH'S CORNER:

What went well in the session?

What challenges came up (for me or my client)?

What could I have done better or in what way can I improve?

What do I need to do to be prepared for next session?

Next session details: DATE: TIME:

NOTES

Made in the USA
Middletown, DE
05 October 2023